W9-DIL-244

The
AMERICAN
HERITAGE®

dic·tion·ar·y

Define·a·Thon™

FOR THE

HIGH

SCHOOL

FRESHMAN

Houghton Mifflin

BOSTON · NEW YORK

Visit our websites: www.ahdictionary.com *or*
www.houghtonmifflinbooks.com

Library of Congress Cataloging-in-Publication Data

The American Heritage Dictionary define-a-thon for the high school freshman.
    p. cm.
  ISBN-13: 978-0-618-44501-1
  ISBN-10: 0-618-44501-3
  1. Vocabulary--Study and teaching (Secondary) I. Title: Define-a-thon for
the high school freshman.
  LB1631.A49 2007
  428.1071'2--dc22

                                                            2007014625

Text design by Anne Chalmers
Typefaces: Memphis, Minion, Frutiger

Manufactured in the United States of America

EB 10 9 8 7 6 5 4 3 2 1

Contents

Staff   iv
Preface   v
Guide to the Define-α-Thon   vii

Define-α-Thon
Word Challenge
1

Define-α-Thon
Word Challenge
R E V E A L E D
15

Define-α-Thon
Answer Key
87

Preface

The editors of the American Heritage dictionaries
are pleased to present *The American Heritage Dictionary Define-a-Thon for the High School Freshman*, a new kind of brainteaser that will challenge
students to reach for a more sophisticated vocabulary while at the same time bolstering their dictionary skills to foster more independent learning.

The challenge is both simple and subtle. Each
question consists of a definition and four candidate
words, only one of which is correct. The editors
have carefully selected both the definitions and the
words listed beneath them with the high school
freshman in mind, since all the words can be found
in the reading and curriculum at this level of
school. The words are often similar in sound or
form to one another, so the student must think not
only about the correct choice to each question but
also about the meaning of the other choices as
well. Caution: words can be deceptive!

Define-a-Thon for the High School Freshman is
more than a quiz book, however. It's also a platform
for learning about words. The Word Challenge Revealed section that follows the Word Challenge itself provides fascinating background information
about each correct word, while also explaining
what the other words in the group mean. Each correct word is shown in an example sentence and ac-
companied by an etymology explaining the histori-

cal development of the word, which usually comes from another language such as Latin, Greek, or German. The etymology provides deeper insight into the meaning of the word and can be a helpful aid to remembering what the word means in English today.

Some words have remarkable stories that can't be conveyed easily in an etymology. These stories are told in separate paragraphs and make for fascinating reading. For some words, still more help appears in the form of quotations from authors who are typically read during the first year of high school. If these famous authors liked and used these words, why shouldn't you?

The editors of the American Heritage dictionaries encourage you to incorporate the words presented in this book into your own vocabulary. The more powerful your vocabulary becomes, the easier it will be for you to express what you are thinking clearly and effectively—wherever you may be.

So take up the Define-a-Thon challenge and make yourself a better student! No matter how you play—alone, with friends, or with family—you are sure to end up a winner!

— Joe Pickett
Executive Editor
— Steve Kleinedler
Supervising Editor

Guide to the Define-a-Thon

The first part of the book, the Define-a-Thon Word
Challenge, consists of a series of definitions. Each
definition is followed by four possible answers.
Only one of these answers is correct. It is your job
to determine the correct answer.

The second part, the Define-a-Thon Word Challenge
Revealed, is much more than an answer key. It provides you with a wealth of information about the
words used in the Define-a-Thon. For each word that
is the correct answer, we provide a sentence to show
how this word is used in context. Additionally, we
show the etymology of the word, so you can learn
how this word entered the English language and
how it might be related to other words. If an etymology contains a word that is not actually preserved in
written documents but that scholars are confident
did exist, such a form is marked by an asterisk (*).
We also provide the definition for each word that is
an incorrect answer, so you can learn the meanings
of all the words and see how they differ.

Some entries include notes that present interesting
information regarding the history or meaning of the
word. Other entries include quotations from works
of literature to show how well-established writers

have used the word in both classic and contemporary texts. Following the Define-a-Thon Word Challenge Revealed is a simple answer key that lists the correct answers at a glance.

Reading and understanding this material is a fun and easy way to incorporate useful new words into your active vocabulary.

Define-a-Thon
Word Challenge

1. To enclose completely with or as if with a covering; wrap up.

endeavor   enhance

enthrall   envelop

2. A very steep mass of rock, as a cliff.

precedent   precipice

prestige   prism

3. The condition of living or lasting forever.

immortality   impatience

impression   impurity

4. Required by law or a rule.

compatible   compulsory

consecutive   conspicuous

5. To cut small bits or shavings from wood with a knife.

flatter   tattle

twitter   whittle

6. Something that gets in the way of something else; a blockage.

construction   destruction

instruction   obstruction

7. To begin or cause to begin to grow; sprout.

coordinate   culminate

exterminate   germinate

8. One of the tiny blood vessels that connect the smallest arteries to the smallest veins.

capillary   caravan

cargo   cascade

9. To say more on a subject; give details.

elaborate   elevate

evaporate   exhilarate

10. Happening or existing at the same time.

clockwise   simultaneous

timid   wishful

11. The photographic record of a three-dimensional image that has been produced by using a divided beam of light from a laser.

hologram   monogram

parallelogram   telegram

12. Either of the two times of the year when day and night are equal in length everywhere on the earth and the sun appears to shine directly above the equator.

annex   equinox

index   sphinx

13. Betrayal of one's country, especially by waging war against it or giving aid to an enemy.

assault   perjury

slander   treason

14. The Japanese art of folding paper into complicated designs and shapes.

casserole   kimono

origami   oriole

15. To light up; shine light on.

illuminate   immigrate

invigorate   irrigate

16. Relating to the prevention of disease and the protection of health.

hereditary	momentary
sanitary	solitary

17. To put out a fire or flame.

anguish	distinguish
extinguish	languish

18. The equipment used in or associated with some activity.

panorama	paraphernalia
partition	pavilion

19. Eager to succeed or to gain fame or power.

ambitious	amiable
ample	animated

20. To be a regular customer of.

criticize	hypnotize
jeopardize	patronize

21. Of greatest importance or concern; primary.

parallel   paramount

parochial   particular

22. The specialized or technical language of a trade, profession, or similar group.

cauldron   jargon

mention   paragon

23. Capable of containing a large quantity; roomy.

capacious   gracious

judicious   pernicious

24. Rules that tell people how to behave in social situations.

eloquence   etiquette

masquerade   tourniquet

25. To turn aside from a main issue or course.

capsize   overturn

revolve   sidetrack

26. Feeling or showing doubt.

aggrieved   dubious

heartbroken   thankless

27. Transmitting light, but scattering it enough so that images become blurred or are indistinct.

transcendent   transitory

translucent   transparent

28. The scientific study of animals.

anthropology   ecology

etymology   zoology

29. A system of symbols or figures used to represent things such as numbers or musical tones.

notation   population

resignation   variation

30. Able to do many things well.

adverse   controversial

perverse   versatile

31. To move with light, running steps; scamper.

creep   fidget

scurry   wriggle

32. A place to which someone is going or to which something is sent.

congregation   destination

dissipation   simulation

33. A place of refuge, asylum, or protection.

estuary   infatuation

obituary   sanctuary

34. To take something away from someone, in some cases by legal authority.

concentrate   confiscate

congratulate   consolidate

35. A practice, such as washing the hands, or a condition, such as clean water, that aids good health.

exercise   goodwill

hygiene   welfare

36. Slanting from one corner of a four-sided figure, as a square, to another corner.

adjacent   diagonal

parallel   zigzag

37. To declare to be true without offering proof.

allege   condemn

deny   proclaim

38. To ask earnestly; beg.

entreat   maltreat

retreat   treat

39. Wild confusion and noise; uproar.

explosion   muffler

pandemonium   percussion

40. An animal that has no backbone.

invertebrate   mammal

quadruped   reptile

41. Friendly and generous to guests; cordial.

    charitable   hospitable

    pliable   unreliable

42. Peaceful and calm.

    clamorous   serene

    succinct   verbose

43. The most basic unit of an image on a computer or television screen, many of which are arranged in rows and columns and are lit up in a specific pattern to create an image.

    bar code   icon

    pixel   virus

44. A person from whom one is descended.

    acquaintance   ancestor

    character   offspring

45. To put off until a later time.

    foreshadow   lather

    offset   postpone

46. To turn so that the bottom of something becomes the top; overturn.

capitalize   capsize

captivate   capture

47. The condition of being successful, especially in money matters.

charity   finance

philanthropy   prosperity

48. Going beyond the limits of reason; excessive.

extracurricular   extraterrestrial

extravagant   extrinsic

49. A unit of length in the metric system equal to 1,000 meters.

centimeter   decameter

kilometer   millimeter

50. Full of energy; lively.

conventional   expansive

strenuous   vigorous

51. To continue to try to do something despite obstacles or difficulties.

persevere   preserve

reserve   sever

52. A musical instrument that is made up of two rows of wooden bars of varying lengths.

harpsichord   ukulele

xylophone   zither

53. A machine for lifting and moving heavy objects. It consists of a movable boom that is equipped with pulleys and cables and is connected to the base of a stationary vertical beam.

derrick   dredge

lever   wedge

54. Having no useful results; useless.

disposable   durable

futile   practicable

55. To soak or become soaked.

dampen   mire

saturate   sprinkle

56. Neat and tidy.

> downcast   shipshape
>
> underhanded   wholesome

57. The number written above or to the left of the line in a fraction.

> denominator   division
>
> numerator   product

58. To weaken or destroy the strength or vitality of.

> encourage   energize
>
> enervate   enrage

Define-a-Thon
Word Challenge
R E V E A L E D

A heavy summer fog **enveloped** Kennedy International. The roar of the great planes was silenced but in the airport there was noise and confusion. Adam wandered about, trying not to look lost, keeping one ear open to the blaring of the loudspeaker in case his flight to Lisbon should be called or canceled.

— Madeleine L'Engle
The Arm of the Starfish

1.

envelop

To enclose completely with or as if with a covering; wrap up.

They enveloped the baby in a blanket to protect her from the harsh wind.

[From Middle English *envolupen,* to be involved in, from Old French *envoluper, envoloper* : *en-,* in + *voloper,* to wrap up.]

WHAT THE OTHER WORDS MEAN

endeavor: To make a serious effort; to try earnestly.

enhance: To make greater, as in value or beauty; heighten.

enthrall: To hold as if under a magic spell; fascinate.

precipice

A very steep mass of rock, as a cliff.

*I looked over the edge of the
precipice and saw a river in
the canyon far below.*

[From French *précipice*, from Latin *praecipitium*,
from *praeceps, praecipit-*, headlong : *prae-*, before,
in front + *caput, capit-*, head.]

WHAT THE OTHER WORDS MEAN

precedent: A model or example that may
be followed or referred to later.

prestige: Great respect or importance in
the opinion of others.

prism: A transparent, solid object that
usually has triangular bases
and rectangular sides and
breaks light up into bands of
color.

3.

immortality

The condition of living or lasting forever.

*Death and immortality are
recurrent themes in Emily
Dickinson's poetry.*

[From Middle English, from Old French *immorta-
lité*, from Latin *immortālitās* : *in-*, not + a word
element akin to *mors, mort-*, death and *morī*, to die
+ *-ālis*, adjectival suffix + *-tās*, suffix forming
abstract nouns.]

WHAT THE OTHER WORDS MEAN

impatience: The unwillingness to wait or
put up with something calmly.

impression: An effect, image, or feeling
that stays in the mind.

impurity: The condition of being un-
clean; contamination.

4.

compulsory

Required by law or a rule.

Filing a tax return is compulsory; if you don't do it, you could end up in jail.

[From Latin *compulsor,* compeller, from Latin *compulsus,* past participle of *compellere,* to compel.]

WHAT THE OTHER WORDS MEAN

compatible: Capable of living or existing together in harmony.

consecutive: Following one right after the other.

conspicuous: Attracting notice.

5.

whittle

To cut small bits or shavings from wood with a knife.

When you've finished whittling that stick, please sweep up the shavings.

[From Middle English *whyttel*, knife, variant of *thwitel*, from *thwiten*, to whittle, from Old English *thwītan*, to strike, whittle down.]

WHAT THE OTHER WORDS MEAN

flatter: To praise in a way that is not sincere, especially in order to get something in return.

tattle: To tell someone else's secrets.

twitter: To make high chirping sounds.

6.

obstruction

Something that gets in the way of something else; a blockage.

A large boulder fell from the cliff onto the road, creating an obstruction that blocked traffic in both directions.

[From Latin *obstrūctiō, obstrūction-*, from *obstruere, obstrūct-*, to wall up, barricade, block : *ob-*, against + *struere*, to pile up.]

WHAT THE OTHER WORDS MEAN

construction: The act or process of building by fitting parts together.

destruction: The act or process of completely ruining something.

instruction: Something that is taught; a lesson or series of lessons.

Then, as the angle of incline lessened, as the mound—*the hill*—flattened, nearing the bottom, the sled's forward motion slowed. The snow was piled now around it, and he pushed with his body, moving it forward, not wanting the exhilarating ride to end.

Finally the **obstruction** of the piled snow was too much for the thin runners of the sled, and he came to a stop. He sat there for a moment, panting, holding the rope in his cold hands.

—Lois Lowry
The Giver

germinate

To begin or cause to begin to grow; sprout.

Seeds need water and warmth to germinate.

[From Latin *germināre, germināt-*, to sprout, from *germen, germin-*, sprout, bud.]

WHAT THE OTHER WORDS MEAN

coordinate: To work or cause to work together easily or well.

culminate: To reach the highest point or degree.

exterminate: To get rid of by destroying completely.

8.

capillary

One of the tiny blood vessels that connect the smallest arteries to the smallest veins.

Looking in the microscope, the doctor could observe red blood cells traveling through the capillaries.

[From Latin *capillāris*, pertaining to hair (because of the hairlike thinness of capillary blood vessels) : *capillus*, hair + *-āris*, adjectival suffix.]

WHAT THE OTHER WORDS MEAN

caravan: A group of people or vehicles that travel together.

cargo: The freight carried by a vehicle such as a ship or an airplane.

cascade: A waterfall or group of waterfalls that flows over steep rocks.

9.

elaborate

To say more on a subject; give details.

During the question-and-answer period, the author elaborated on why she had chosen a dog as the main character of the book.

[From Latin *ēlabōrātus*, past participle of *ēlabōrāre*, to work out : *ē-*, *ex-*, intensive prefix + *labōrāre*, to work (from *labor*, work).]

WHAT THE OTHER WORDS MEAN

elevate: To raise to a higher place, position, or level; lift up.

evaporate: To change into a vapor or gas.

exhilarate: To make cheerful, lively, or full of energy.

simultaneous

Happening or existing at the same time.

When a thunderstorm is directly overhead, the flash of lightning and boom of thunder are simultaneous.

[From Latin *simul*, at the same time + English *-taneous* (as in *instantaneous*).]

WHAT THE OTHER WORDS MEAN

clockwise: In the direction in which the hands of a clock rotate.

timid: Easily frightened; shy.

wishful: Having or showing a wish or desire, often for something that is not likely to happen.

hologram

The photographic record of a three-dimensional image that has been produced by using a divided beam of light from a laser.

The museum had an exhibit of holograms that allowed visitors to view images of different flowers from all sides.

[From Greek *holos-*, whole + *-gramma*, picture, drawing.]

WHAT THE OTHER WORDS MEAN

monogram: A design made by combining the initials of a person's name.

parallelogram: A four-sided figure with parallel opposite sides.

telegram: A message sent that is transmitted by wire or radio to a receiving station.

If you tear an ordinary photograph in two, each piece shows only a part of the original image. If you break a **hologram** in two, each piece shows the entire original scene, although from slightly different points of view. That's because each spot on a hologram contains enough information to show how the entire scene would look if it were viewed from a particular point of view. Imagine looking at a room through a peephole set in a solid door. What you see depends on where in the door the peephole is placed. Each piece of the hologram is a "peephole" view, and that's what makes the image look three-dimensional: as you move the hologram around or look at different parts of it, you see the original object from different angles, just as if you were walking around it. For this reason, holograms are much harder to copy than simple two-dimensional images: to forge one you'd have to know what the original object looked like from many angles. And that's why credit cards and other important items include holographic stickers as indicators of authenticity.

12.

equinox

Either of the two times of the year when day and night are equal in length everywhere on the earth and the sun appears to shine directly above the equator.

The September equinox marks the beginning of fall in the Northern Hemisphere and of spring in the Southern Hemisphere.

[From Middle English, from Old French *equinoxe*, from Medieval Latin *aequinoxium*, from Latin *aequinoctium : aequi-*, equal + *nox, noct-*, night.]

WHAT THE OTHER WORDS MEAN

annex: A building that is added to or stands near another, bigger building and is used for some related purpose.

index: An alphabetized list of things or persons, used to keep track of them and to find out where they are located.

sphinx: An ancient Egyptian figure with the body of a lion and the head of a man, ram, or hawk.

13.

treason

Betrayal of one's country, especially by waging war against it or giving aid to an enemy.

The spy was charged with treason for sharing state secrets with the enemy.

[From Middle English, from Anglo-Norman *treson*, from Latin *trāditiō, trāditiōn-*, a handing over, from *trādere*, to hand over : *trā-, trāns-*, across + *dare*, to give.]

WHAT THE OTHER WORDS MEAN

assault: An unlawful attempt or threat to injure another physically.

perjury: The deliberate giving of false, misleading, or incomplete testimony while under oath.

slander: The act or crime of reporting or uttering a false statement maliciously to damage someone's reputation.

14.

origami

The Japanese art of folding paper into complicated designs and shapes.

I asked my friend who is skilled in origami to show me how to fold the square of paper into the shape of a bird.

[From Japanese *origami* : *ori*, verbal noun of *oru*, to fold + *kami*, paper.]

WHAT THE OTHER WORDS MEAN

casserole: A dish, usually made of pottery or glass, in which food is baked and served.

kimono: A long, loose robe with wide sleeves and a broad sash, traditionally worn by the Japanese as an outer garment.

oriole: A songbird that has black and yellow or black and orange feathers in the male.

illuminate

To light up; shine light on.

Even though it was the middle of the night, the hikers had no trouble following the path, which was illuminated by the full moon.

[From Middle English *illuminaten,* from Latin *illūmināre, illūmināt-* : *in-,* in + *lūmināre,* to light up (from *lūmen, lūmin-,* light).]

WHAT THE OTHER WORDS MEAN

immigrate: To come into a foreign country to live.

invigorate: To give energy or strength to.

irrigate: To supply with water by means of a system of ditches, pipes, and canals.

sanitary

Relating to the prevention of disease and the protection of health.

Washing your hands before eating is a good sanitary practice.

[From French *sanitaire*, from Latin *sānitās*, health, from *sānus*, healthy.]

WHAT THE OTHER WORDS MEAN

hereditary: Passed on from parent to off-spring.

momentary: Lasting only for a short time.

solitary: Being alone; not with others.

extinguish

To put out a fire or flame.

I extinguished the fire by pouring a bucket of water on it.

[From Latin *exstinguere* : *ex-*, intensive prefix + *stinguere*, to quench.]

WHAT THE OTHER WORDS MEAN

anguish: To feel or suffer agonizing physical or mental pain.

distinguish: To recognize as being different or distinct.

languish: To lose strength or vigor; grow weak.

The original **paraphernalia** for the lottery had been lost long ago, and the black box now resting on the stool had been put into use even before Old Man Warner, the oldest man in town, was born. Mr. Summers spoke frequently to the villagers about making a new box, but no one liked to upset even as much tradition as was represented by the black box.

—Shirley Jackson
"The Lottery"

18.

paraphernalia

The equipment used in or associated with some activity.

A baseball team's paraphernalia includes mitts, bats, balls, and bases.

[From Medieval Latin *paraphernālia*, neuter plural of *paraphernālis*, pertaining to the *parapherna*, a married woman's property exclusive of her dowry, from Greek : *para-*, beyond + *phernē*, dowry.]

WHAT THE OTHER WORDS MEAN

panorama: A view or picture of everything that can be seen over a wide area.

partition: Something, as a partial wall, that divides up a room or space.

pavilion: A building with open sides that is used at parks or fairs.

19.

ambitious

Eager to succeed or to gain fame or power.

The ambitious mountain climber decided to lead an expedition to scale Mount Everest.

[From Middle English *ambicious,* from Old French *ambitieux* and Latin *ambitiōsus,* from Latin *ambitiō, ambitiōn-,* going around canvassing for votes, ostentation, from *ambitus,* past participle of *ambīre,* to go around.]

WHAT THE OTHER WORDS MEAN

amiable: Friendly and pleasant; good-natured.

ample: More than enough; plenty of.

animated: Full of life or spirit; lively.

patronize

To be a regular customer of.

That restaurant has the best pancakes in town, so I patronize it frequently.

[From *patron* (from Middle English, from Old French, from Latin *patrōnus*, from *pater*, *patr-*, father) + *-ize*, verbal suffix.]

WHAT THE OTHER WORDS MEAN

criticize: To judge the good and bad qualities of; evaluate.

hypnotize: To put someone into a relaxed, sleeplike, but alert state.

jeopardize: To put someone or something in danger.

paramount

Of greatest importance or concern; primary.

Her paramount task is to regain the strength in her broken leg.

[From Anglo-Norman *paramont,* above : *par,* by (from Latin *per*) + *amont,* above, upward (from Latin *ad montem,* to the hill: *ad,* to + *mōns, mont-,* hill).]

WHAT THE OTHER WORDS MEAN

parallel: Lying in the same plane and being the same distance apart at all points.

parochial: Limited in range or understanding; narrow.

particular: Relating to a single, specific person or thing.

jargon

The specialized or technical language of a trade, profession, or similar group.

The doctors were advised to use simple words instead of medical jargon when speaking with their patients.

[From Middle English *jargoun*, from Old French *jargon*, probably of imitative origin.]

WHAT THE OTHER WORDS MEAN

cauldron: A large kettle for boiling.

mention: The act of referring to something briefly or casually.

paragon: A model of excellence; a perfect example.

23.

capacious

Capable of containing a large quantity; roomy.

*The capacious auditorium
seats over 600 people.*

[From Latin *capāx, capāc-,* from *capere,* to take.]

WHAT THE OTHER WORDS MEAN

gracious: Courteous and kind.

judicious: Having or showing good sense
or judgment.

pernicious: Very harmful or destructive.

The houses were as handsome and as unusual as I remembered. Clever modernizations of old Colonial manses, extensions in Victorian wood, **capacious** Greek Revival temples lined the street, as impressive and just as forbidding as ever. I had rarely seen anyone go into one of them, or anyone playing on a lawn, or even an open window.

—John Knowles
A Separate Peace

etiquette

Rules that tell people how to behave in social situations.

It is good etiquette to give up your seat on the bus for an older person.

[From French, from Old French *estiquet*, label.]

WHAT THE OTHER WORDS MEAN

eloquence: The skill of using clear, forceful, and effective language.

masquerade: A party or dance at which people wear masks and fancy costumes.

tourniquet: A device, such as a tightly twisted bandage, used to stop bleeding.

25.

sidetrack

To turn aside from a main issue or course.

The discussion in our biology class became sidetracked when we started talking about circus elephants.

[From *sidetrack*, a railroad siding, railroad track going off the main line.]

WHAT THE OTHER WORDS MEAN

capsize: To turn so that the bottom of something becomes the top; overturn.

overturn: To tip or turn something over.

revolve: To orbit a central point.

26.

dubious

Feeling or showing doubt.

I was dubious as to whether I'd ever finish knitting the sweater.

[From Latin *dubius*.]

WHAT THE OTHER WORDS MEAN

aggrieved: Feeling unhappy or troubled.

heartbroken: Feeling great sorrow or sadness.

thankless: Not feeling or showing gratitude.

translucent

Transmitting light, but scattering it enough so that images become blurred or are indistinct.

The office door was made of translucent glass, so you couldn't see clearly who was inside.

[From Latin *trānslūcēns*, *trānslūcent-*, present participle of *trānslūcēre*, to shine through : *trāns-*, across + *lūcēre*, to shine.]

WHAT THE OTHER WORDS MEAN

transcendent: Surpassing others; preeminent or supreme.

transitory: Existing or lasting only briefly; short-lived.

transparent: Capable of transmitting light so that objects and images are clearly visible, as if there were nothing between the observer and the light source.

28.

zoology

The scientific study of animals.

The park ranger has a degree in zoology.

[From New Latin *zōologia* : Greek *zōion*, living being + *-logiā*, study, theory (from *logos*, word, speech, and *legein*, to speak).]

WHAT THE OTHER WORDS MEAN

anthropology: The scientific study of the origin, the behavior, and the physical, social, and cultural development of humans.

ecology: The science that deals with the relationships among organisms and between organisms and their environment.

etymology: The history of a word, including where it or its parts came from and how it got its present form and meaning.

Traditionally, the first syllable of **zoology** has been pronounced as (zō), rhyming with *toe*. However, most likely due to the familiarity of the word zoo (which is merely a shortened form of *zoological garden*), the pronunciation of the first syllable as zoo is also commonly heard.

notation

A system of symbols or figures used to represent things such as numbers or musical tones.

Because I knew musical notation, I was able to write the melody down after my friend sang it for me.

[From Latin *notātiō*, *notātiōn-*, from *notātus*, past participle of *notāre*, to note, from *nota*, note.]

WHAT THE OTHER WORDS MEAN

population: The total number of people living in a certain place.

resignation: The act of giving up or quitting a position.

variation: A change from the normal or usual.

30.

versatile

Able to do many things well.

*You are such a versatile athlete—
not many people are good at baseball, basketball, and football, too.*

[From Latin *versātilis*, able to turn around,
movable, versatile, from *versātus*, past participle of
versāre, to turn.]

WHAT THE OTHER WORDS MEAN

adverse: Not favorable; hostile.

controversial: Causing argument or debate.

perverse: Showing stubbornness or con-
trariness.

scurry

To move with light, running steps; scamper.

*The mice scurried across the
kitchen floor.*

[Probably ultimately a back-formation from
scurrier, scout, rider sent out to reconnoiter an area,
from Middle English *scurrour,* probably from Old
French *descouvreor,* discoverer, from *descouvrir,* to
discover.]

WHAT THE OTHER WORDS MEAN

creep: To move slowly with the body
close to the ground.

fidget: To move in a nervous or rest-
less way.

wriggle: To turn or twist the body with
winding, writhing motions;
squirm.

32.

destination

A place to which someone is going or to which something is sent.

The destination of this flight is O'Hare International Airport in Chicago.

[From Latin *dēstinātiō, dēstinātion-*, determination, resolution, from *dēstināre, dēstināt-*, to determine, resolve.]

WHAT THE OTHER WORDS MEAN

congregation: A group of people gathered for religious worship.

dissipation: The act of scattering or the condition of being scattered.

simulation: An imitation or a false appearance.

A howl rose from the kitchen, reminding Tibby of two other unproductive creatures in the house—her two-year-old brother and one-year-old sister. They were all noise and destruction and evil-smelling diapers. Even Wallman's drugstore seemed like a **sanctuary** compared to her house at lunchtime.

—Ann Brashares
The Sisterhood of the Traveling Pants

33.

sanctuary

A place of refuge, asylum, or protection.

The rebels used the cathedral as a sanctuary from the king's soldiers.

[From Middle English, from Old French *sainctuarie*, from Late Latin *sānctuārium*, from Latin *sānctus*, sacred.]

WHAT THE OTHER WORDS MEAN

estuary: The wide lower part of a river where its current is met by the tides of the ocean.

infatuation: A foolish, unreasoning, or extravagant passion or attraction.

obituary: A printed notice of a person's death, often with a short biography.

confiscate

To take something away from someone,
in some cases by legal authority.

*The teacher will confiscate your
cell phone if it rings during class.*

[From Latin *cōnfiscāre, cōnfiscāt-* : *com-*, together,
with + *fiscus,* treasury.]

WHAT THE OTHER WORDS MEAN

concentrate: To keep or direct one's
thoughts, attention, or efforts
on something.

congratulate: To give praise or good wishes
to someone at a happy event or
for something done well.

consolidate: To join together into one.

hygiene

A practice, such as washing the hands, or a condition, such as clean water, that aids good health.

When the villagers started using proper hygiene, rates of disease decreased.

[From French *hygiène* and New Latin *hygieina*, both from Greek *hugieinē (tekhnē)*, (art) of health, feminine of *hugieinos*, relating to health, from *hugiēs*, healthy.]

WHAT THE OTHER WORDS MEAN

exercise: Physical activity for the good of the body.

goodwill: A kindly or friendly attitude.

welfare: Health, happiness, or prosperity; well-being.

diagonal

Slanting from one corner of a four-sided figure, as a square, to another corner.

We took a diagonal path across the park, which was shorter than walking along its sides.

[From Latin *diagōnālis*, from Greek *diagōnios*, from angle to angle : *dia-*, through + *gōniā*, angle, corner.]

WHAT THE OTHER WORDS MEAN

adjacent: Next to or close to.

parallel: Lying in the same plane and being the same distance apart at all points.

zigzag: Moving in a line that runs first one way and then another in a series of short, sharp turns.

allege

To declare to be true without offering proof.

> *The lawyer alleged that the defendant had stolen the car, but he said he was innocent.*

[From Middle English *alleggen,* to make a formal declaration in court, from Old French *alegier,* to vindicate, justify (influenced by *aleguer,* to give a reason), from *esligier,* to pay a fine, justify oneself, from Vulgar Latin *exlītigāre,* to clear at law : Latin *ex-,* out + Latin *lītigāre,* to sue (from *līs, līt-,* lawsuit + *agere,* to drive, conduct).]

WHAT THE OTHER WORDS MEAN

condemn: To declare someone guilty and say what the punishment is.

deny: To declare to be not true.

proclaim: To announce publicly; declare.

38.

entreat

To ask earnestly; beg.

I entreated my friends to go to the dance with me.

[From Middle English *entreten,* to deal with, negotiate, plead with, from Anglo-Norman *entreter* : *en-,* intensive prefix + *treter,* to treat (from Latin *tractāre,* to handle, manage, frequentative of *trahere,* to drag).]

WHAT THE OTHER WORDS MEAN

maltreat: To treat in a rough or cruel way; abuse.

retreat: To go backward or recede from a position or condition that has been gained.

treat: To regard and handle in a certain way.

Two of the fairest stars in all the heaven,

Having some business, do **entreat** her eyes

To twinkle in their spheres till they return.

What if her eyes were there, they in her head?

The brightness of her cheek would shame
     those stars,

As daylight doth a lamp; her eyes in heaven

Would through the airy region stream so bright

That birds would sing and think it were not
     night.

> —William Shakespeare
> *The Tragedy of Romeo and Juliet*
> (Act 2, Scene 2)

pandemonium

Wild confusion and noise; uproar.

When the gorilla escaped, it created pandemonium at the zoo.

[From *Pandæmonium,* name given to the capital of Hell in the epic poem *Paradise Lost* by John Milton (1608–1674) : Greek *pan-,* all + Late Latin *daemonium,* demon (from Greek *daimonion,* from *daimōn,* lesser god, demon).]

WHAT THE OTHER WORDS MEAN

explosion: The act of bursting apart suddenly with great force and noise.

muffler: A device that deadens the noise of a motor vehicle's engine.

percussion: The striking together of two things, especially when it creates noise.

40.

invertebrate

An animal that has no backbone.

Worms, clams, insects, and lobsters are all examples of invertebrates.

[From New Latin *invertebrātus* : Latin *in-*, not + *vertebrātus*, having joints (from *vertebra*, joint, vertebra, from *vertere*, to turn).]

WHAT THE OTHER WORDS MEAN

mammal: Any of various warm-blooded animals that have a backbone, hair or fur, and, in the females, mammary glands that produce milk for feeding their young.

quadruped: An animal having four feet, such as most reptiles and mammals.

reptile: Any of various cold-blooded animals, such as snakes, turtles, and crocodiles, that have a backbone, are covered with scales or horny plates, and breathe by means of lungs.

41.

hospitable

Friendly and generous to guests; cordial.

*The gracious and hospitable host
made sure all of the guests had
plenty to eat.*

[From obsolete French *hospitable*, ultimately from Latin
hospitāre, to put up as a guest, from *hospes, hospit-*,
guest, host.]

WHAT THE OTHER WORDS MEAN

charitable: Generous in giving money or
other help to needy people.

pliable: Easily bent or shaped without
breaking; flexible.

unreliable: Not to be depended on or
trusted.

42.

serene

Peaceful and calm.

There was a serene look on the sleeping child's face.

[From Middle English, from Latin *serēnus,* serene, clear.]

WHAT THE OTHER WORDS MEAN

clamorous: Loud and noisy.

succinct: Characterized by clear, precise expression in few words; concise.

verbose: Using or containing more words than necessary; wordy.

43.

pixel

The most basic unit of an image on a computer or television screen, many of which are arranged in rows and columns and are lit up in a specific pattern to create an image.

The large screen contained millions of pixels.

[From *pix* (variant spelling of *pics*, the plural of *pic*, short for *picture*) + *el(ement)*.]

WHAT THE OTHER WORDS MEAN

bar code: A series of vertical bars that are printed on a product and can be read by a computer scanner.

icon: A small picture on a computer screen that represents something stored in the computer, such as a data file or a software program.

virus: A computer program that copies itself into the other programs stored in a computer, often causing damage to those programs or to other data.

If you look at a panel in a comic book very closely, you will see that colored or shaded areas are often made of very tiny dots. Images on computer screens are also composed of very tiny dots, known as **pixels.** (*Pixel* is a shortening of *picture element*.) Each color on a computer screen is made of an arrangement of red, blue, and green pixels that vary in intensity. Most monitors have hundreds of thousands to millions of pixels. Each pixel is lit or dimmed individually to create an image. Screens with the smallest pixels have the sharpest images, but they require more computer memory to store data about the color and intensity of each pixel.

44.

ancestor

A person from whom one is descended.

My ancestors came to the United States from Italy and Greece in the 1880s.

[From Middle English *auncestre*, from Old French, from Latin *antecessor*, predecessor, from *antecessus*, past participle of *antecēdere*, to precede : *ante-*, before + *cēdere*, to go.]

WHAT THE OTHER WORDS MEAN

acquaintance: A person whom one knows.

character: A person or figure in a story, book, play, or movie.

offspring: The young of a person, animal, or plant.

postpone

To put off until a later time.

We decided to postpone the parade until next Saturday because of rain.

[From Latin *postpōnere* : *post-*, after + *pōnere*, to put.]

WHAT THE OTHER WORDS MEAN

foreshadow: To present an indication or a suggestion of beforehand.

lather: To cover with a thick, creamy foam made by mixing soap and water.

offset: To counterbalance or counteract; make up for.

capsize

To turn so that the bottom of something becomes the top; overturn.

The large waves struck the boat from the side and caused it to capsize.

[Perhaps from Spanish *capuzar* or Catalan *cabussar*, to push (someone's) head underwater, ultimately from Latin *caput*, head.]

WHAT THE OTHER WORDS MEAN

capitalize: To begin with a capital letter.

captivate: To fascinate or charm, as with intelligence or beauty.

capture: To get hold of, as by force or craft; seize.

prosperity

The condition of being successful, especially in money matters.

Because of the wealthy couple's prosperity, they were able to provide the funds to build a new wing for the library.

[From Middle English *prosperite*, from Old French, from Latin *prosperitās*, from *prosperus*, favorable : *prō*, for, just as + a word element akin to Latin *spēs*, hope.]

WHAT THE OTHER WORDS MEAN

charity: The giving of money or other help to needy people.

finance: The management and use of money, especially by government, banks, and businesses.

philanthropy: The desire or effort to help humankind, as by making charitable donations.

The animals were not badly off throughout the summer, in spite of the hardness of their work. If they had no more food than they had had in Jones's day, at least they did not have less. The advantage of only having to feed themselves, and not having to support five **extravagant** human beings as well, was so great that it would have taken a lot of failures to outweigh it. And in many ways the animal method of doing things was more efficient and saved labour.

—George Orwell
Animal Farm

extravagant

Going beyond the limits of reason; excessive.

They flew all the guests to Hawaii for an extravagant wedding at a resort on the beach.

[From Middle English *extravagant,* unusual, rambling, from Old French, from Medieval Latin *extrāvagāns, extrāvagant-,* present participle of *extrāvagārī,* to wander : Latin *extrā,* outside + Latin *vagārī,* to wander.]

WHAT THE OTHER WORDS MEAN

extracurricular: Being outside the regular course of study of a school or college.

extraterrestrial: Beyond the earth or outside its atmosphere.

extrinsic: Originating from the outside; external.

49.

kilometer

A unit of length in the metric system
equal to 1,000 meters.

> *One mile equals about 1.6
> kilometers.*

[From French *kilomètre* : *kilo-*, thousand (from
Greek *khīlioi*, thousand) + *mètre*, meter (from
Greek *metron*, measure).]

WHAT THE OTHER WORDS MEAN

centimeter: A unit of length in the metric
system equal to one-hundredth
of a meter.

decameter: A unit of length in the metric
system equal to 10 meters.

millimeter: A unit of length in the metric
system equal to one-thousandth
of a meter.

vigorous

Full of energy; lively.

*The vigorous puppy pulled on
the leash as it tried to chase
the squirrel.*

[From Middle English, from Old French *vigourous,*
from Medieval Latin *vigorōsus,* from Latin *vigor,*
liveliness, from *vigēre,* to be lively.]

WHAT THE OTHER WORDS MEAN

conventional: Following accepted practice,
customs, or taste.

expansive: Broad in size or extent; com-
prehensive.

strenuous: Requiring great effort or energy.

persevere

To continue to try to do something despite obstacles or difficulties.

The little boy persevered in his efforts to reach the cookie jar on the top shelf.

[From Middle English *perseveren,* from Old French *perseverer,* from Latin *persevērāre,* from *persevērus,* very serious : *per-*, through, thoroughly + *sevērus,* severe.]

WHAT THE OTHER WORDS MEAN

preserve: To protect, as from injury or destruction.

reserve: To set aside for a special purpose or for later use.

sever: To divide, separate, or keep apart.

xylophone

A musical instrument that is made up of two rows of wooden bars of varying lengths.

A xylophone is played by striking the bars with small wooden hammers.

[From Greek *xulon*, wood + *phonē*, voice, sound.]

WHAT THE OTHER WORDS MEAN

harpsichord: A keyboard instrument that looks like a small piano. A harpsichord's strings are plucked by leather picks or quills rather than struck by hammers.

ukulele: A small guitar that has four strings.

zither: A musical instrument made of a flat box with about 30 to 40 strings stretched across it. A zither is played by plucking the strings with the fingers or a pick.

We crossed the railroad tracks and turned right. In front of us were three or four boxes of sugarcane, waiting to be picked up by a train and taken to the mill. We could also see the weighing scales left of the full boxcars, and the **derrick** that lifted the cane from wagons and trailers and swung it onto the boxcars. Left of the weighing scales and the derrick was the plantation cemetery, where my ancestors had been buried for the past century.

—Ernest J. Gaines
A Lesson Before Dying

derrick

A machine for lifting and moving heavy objects. It consists of a movable boom that is equipped with pulleys and cables and is connected to the base of a stationary vertical beam.

The cargo was hoisted by a derrick and loaded onto the ship.

[From obsolete English *derick*, hangman, gallows, after a 16th-century English hangman named *Derick*.]

WHAT THE OTHER WORDS MEAN

dredge: A machine that removes earth, mud, or silt, as from the bottom of a body of water, by means of a scoop, a series of buckets, or a suction tube.

lever: A simple machine for lifting a weight. A lever consists of a strong, stiff bar that rests on a fixed point on which it turns.

wedge: A block of material, such as wood, that is wide at one end and tapers to a point at the other. A wedge is used for splitting, tightening, or holding things in place.

54.

futile

Having no useful results; useless.

Any attempt to win the baseball game would have been futile because we were behind by 15 runs.

[From Latin *futtilis, fūtilis.*]

WHAT THE OTHER WORDS MEAN

disposable: Made to be thrown away after use.

durable: Capable of withstanding hard wear or long use.

practicable: Capable of being done, carried out, or put into effect; possible.

55.

saturate

To soak or become soaked.

*The heavy storm saturated the
ground with rainwater.*

[From Latin *saturāre, saturāt-*, to fill, from *satur*,
sated.]

WHAT THE OTHER WORDS MEAN

dampen: To make or become slightly
wet.

mire: To cause to sink or become
stuck in or as if in wet, muddy
ground.

sprinkle: To scatter in drops or particles.

56.

shipshape

Neat and tidy.

I made sure everything in the apartment was shipshape before my friends arrived.

[Short for obsolete *shipshapen*, arranged as a ship should be : *ship* + *shapen*, past participle of *shape*.]

WHAT THE OTHER WORDS MEAN

downcast: In low spirits; depressed or sad.

underhanded: Done in a sly or secret way.

wholesome: Good for the health; healthful.

57.

numerator

The number written above or to the left of the line in a fraction.

In the fraction ²/₇, the numerator is 2.

[From French *numérateur* and New Latin *numerātor*, numerator, from Latin *numerātor*, counter, from Latin *numerāre, numerāt-*, to count, from *numerus*, number.]

WHAT THE OTHER WORDS MEAN

denominator: The number written below or to the right of the line in a fraction.

division: The mathematical process of determining how many times one number contains another.

product: The result obtained by multiplying two or more numbers.

58.

enervate

To weaken or destroy the strength or vitality of.

*After lifting weights in the hot gym,
I was completely enervated and
just wanted to take a nap.*

[From Latin *ēnervāre*, *ēnervāt-* : *ē-*, *ex-*, out, without
+ *nervus*, sinew, tendon, nerve.]

WHAT THE OTHER WORDS MEAN

encourage: To give courage, hope, or confidence to.

energize: To give energy to; make active.

enrage: To make extremely angry.

Contrary to what many people think, the verb **enervate** does not mean "to invigorate, energize." In fact, *enervate* means essentially the opposite of *energize*. That's because *enervate* comes from the Latin word *nervus*, "sinew." *Enervate* thus means "to cause to become 'out of muscle,'" that is, "to weaken or sap of strength."

Define-a-Thon
Answer Key

1. envelop
2. precipice
3. immortality
4. compulsory
5. whittle
6. obstruction
7. germinate
8. capillary
9. elaborate
10. simultaneous
11. hologram
12. equinox
13. treason
14. origami
15. illuminate
16. sanitary
17. extinguish
18. paraphernalia
19. ambitious
20. patronize
21. paramount
22. jargon
23. capacious
24. etiquette
25. sidetrack
26. dubious
27. translucent
28. zoology
29. notation
30. versatile
31. scurry
32. destination
33. sanctuary
34. confiscate
35. hygiene
36. diagonal
37. allege
38. entreat
39. pandemonium
40. invertebrate
41. hospitable
42. serene
43. pixel
44. ancestor
45. postpone
46. capsize
47. prosperity
48. extravagant
49. kilometer
50. vigorous
51. persevere
52. xylophone
53. derrick
54. futile
55. saturate
56. shipshape
57. numerator
58. enervate